This is a very special book. Why? Because it's all about YOU!

Since it's your story, you can write or draw in the empty white boxes in the book. (A grown-up can help if you want.)

And don't worry if something doesn't turn out quite perfectly... that's what makes it special!

Read, draw, talk, laugh and have fun!

D1441827

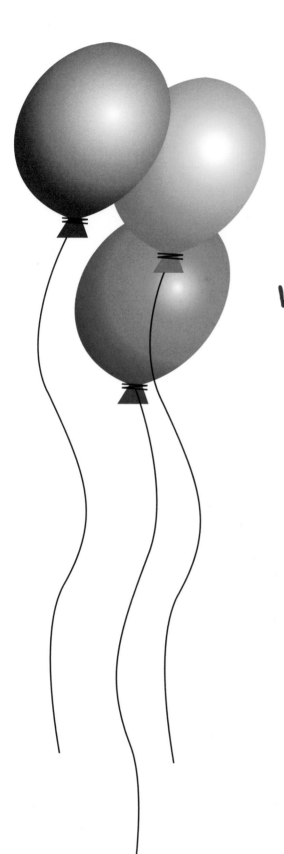

With love to Halia and Kylie
~ Mimi

READ TOGETHER · DO TOGETHER™

Lucky to Live in Colorado

By Kate B. Jerome

Illustrations by Roger Radtke

ARCADIA KIDS

Colorado is home—and I think quite a lot
that I'm lucky to live in this wonderful spot.
Why is it special? That's easy to see.
It's the place that begins the whole story of me!

A picture of me

by

You

Age

Colorado roots keep me strong and it's really quite **neat** that the place they begin is my very own street.

CO

US Map

Where I live

It's close to

Colorado is in the western part of the United States.

Saying welcome to **neighbors** is such fun to do.
Taking time for a chat helps me learn something new.

Colorado hospitality is hard to beat!

Glad you are here!

Please join us!

How interesting! The state butterfly of Colorado is the Colorado Hairstreak Butterfly!

Finding pals is not hard when you share common ground.
Sometimes friends are quite close if you just **look around**.

Good Friends!

is my favorite thing to do.

Colorado **cooks** are so skilled they can please any guest.
(No surprise that they think homemade food is the **best**.)

Rainbow Trout

Green Chile

I love to eat

_____ .

I didn't think I would like

_____

...but I do!

Have you ever tried a
Buffalo burger?

Taking trips to the **park** makes me want to see more.
I have quite a long list of fun things to **explore**.

Colorado Trip List

• Rocky Mountain National Park

• Denver Museum of Nature and Science

• Mesa Verde National Park

It was
fun to visit

Next up:

Can't wait to start packing!

In this state we make **noise** for our favorite home teams.
Win or lose—all great plays deserve very loud **screams**.

SCORE!   YAY!

My Team

Go ahead! Color the T-shirt in your team colors!

Colorado land provides homes for more **critters** than me.
So it's good to **protect** even what we can't see.

Please Don't Pollute!

Some of my favorite animals:

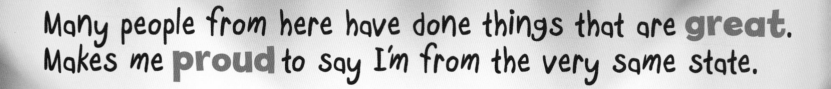

Many people from here have done things that are **great**.
Makes me **proud** to say I'm from the very same state.

WILMA J. WEBB
(State Representative/Community
Leader ~ Denver)

M. SCOTT CARPENTER
(Navy Pilot/NASA Astronaut ~ Boulder)

RUTH HANDLER
(Businesswoman/Inventor ~ Denver)

JOHN KERRY
(Former U.S. Secretary of
State ~ Aurora)

COLORADO BORN

CONGRATULATIONS TO MY HERO

I think

_____

is great because

_____

.

And guess what? You don't have to be famous to be a hero!

In Colorado good **music** will send out a beat
that will start in your ears but end up in your **feet!**

Songs I like to sing:

Colorado has two state songs! "Where the Columbines Grow" was the first one. John Denver's "Rocky Mountain High" was the second.

Colorado people take pride in the things they **create**.
Bright ideas **shine** through from all over the state.

I'm pretty
good at making

In this state **celebrations** are always great fun.
People **laughing** and sharing is just how it's done.

Colorado became a state on August 1, 1876!

My favorite celebration is

because

As my own **story** grows I will never forget
all the places I've been and the **people** I've met.
Yes, the **memories** I have of this wonderful place
are the ones that will always bring **smiles** to my face.

When I grow up I'd like to

Keep exploring! Keep learning! Keep growing!

My Family Tree

Me

Colorado Roots!

A tracing of my hand

My Time Capsule

Things you need:

- a cardboard box (big enough to fit this book and some other small things)
- one blank piece of paper and an envelope
- three index cards
- some favorite little "stuff" (like pictures, artwork, something that shows your favorite team on it)
- a recent newspaper
- tape and some ribbon

First: Fill out two of the index cards. On one, describe your perfect day. On the other, list the price of some things you often use or do.

My perfect day is when...

Milk costs
_____

A Movie ticket costs
_____

Next: Use the blank piece of paper to write a letter to your future self! When you are done, put it in the envelope and seal it shut.

Dear Future Me,
When I think about you in the future I wonder...

Then: Put the index cards, this book, the letter to your future self and the other special "stuff" in the box. Wrap it like a present with the newspaper. Put ribbon around it. Then write on the last index card: DO NOT OPEN FOR 10 YEARS! and tape it to the box.

Finally: Put the box in the back of a closet or somewhere where you won't see it too much. Then wait ten years... and OPEN!

The countdown is starting!

Written by Kate B. Jerome
Illustrations by Roger Radtke
(additional art on page 10 by Sean O'Neill)
Design and Production: Lumina Datamatics, Inc.
Research: Lisa A. Boehm

Published by Arcadia Kids, a division of Arcadia Publishing and
The History Press, Charleston, SC

For all general information contact Arcadia Publishing at:
Telephone: 843-853-2070
Email: sales@arcadiapublishing.com

For Customer Service and Orders:
Toll Free: 1-888-313-2665
Visit us on the internet at
www.arcadiapublishing.com

Library of Congress Cataloging-in-Publication data is
on file with the publisher.

Printed in China